SOTER

1

First Edition—November 2021
Second Reprint—January 2022

MONASTERY OF SAINT MACARIUS THE GREAT
P.O. Box 2780
Cairo—Egypt
E-mail: info@stmacariuspress.com
Phone: +201282211923

USA MAILING ADDRESS:
13303 Scotch Run Ct
Centreville, VA 20120-6428
United States of America

MATTHEW THE POOR

LOVE TOOK FLESH

NATIVITY LETTERS

Edition and Translation from Arabic by

Monks from the Monastery of St. Macarius

ST MACARIUS PRESS

MONASTERY OF SAINT MACARIUS THE GREAT (EGYPT)

ISBN
978-1-7350713-4-3
Library of Congress Control Number
2021949130
Series
Soteria
Translation from Arabic and Editing
Monks from the Monastery of St. Macarius
Illustration
Kirollos Kilada
Cover
David Georgy
Format
5" x 8"
Pages
117

Contents

Introduction

And without controversy great is the mystery of godliness: God was manifested in the flesh, justified in the Spirit, seen by angels, preached among the Gentiles, believed on in the world, received up in glory (1 Tim. 3:16).

We have all encountered the story of Christ's Nativity in various ways throughout the Christmas season. It is presented to us mostly through nativity scenes, television broadcasts, storybooks, paintings, and Christmas performances. In fact, it is not uncommon for Christians nowadays to draw and build their understandings and beliefs on the Nativity from these avenues. In doing so, it unfortunately provides a vague and distorted image of the Nativity's reality and its seminal relation to the history of humanity. The Nativity occurred inside the history of mankind but indeed transcends it. Many preach about Christmas as no more than a mere joyful season of the year (certainly it is) and encourage their hearers to give alms and help the less fortunate. Others may only preach that the Lord has humbled Himself without further elaboration.

Father Matthew the Poor (1919-2006), a Coptic monk and former spiritual father for the monks of Saint Macarius the Great's Monastery in Egypt, offers a different theme and approach to the Nativity. As he eloquently frames God's manifestation in the flesh, "we are the object of Bethlehem." He delves into the Father's heart and rediscovers how He loved the world, to the extent of laying down His only begotten Son *for our sake*. The author never overlooks the fact that the rational creation is at the center of the Father's love. All that we need to do is to agree, accept, and take our role in this salvific path, which is simply wearing the garb of Christ. This garment may entail suffering, poverty, and estrangement, but indeed it will result for us in glory, honor, exultation, and resurrection akin to Christ. We will become aware that we are part of the Nativity and partakers of its outcomes. In simple, we are at the locus of the Nativity. Only when we realize this, we will truly sing the angelic chant, "Glory to God in the Highest, peace on earth and goodwill toward men" (Luke 2:14).

In this compilation, Father Matthew's correspondence with his monks, who at the time were living in the caves of *Wādī al-Rayyān,*[1] focuses on Christ's birth. He encourages his disciples to experience the Father's love for the whole world, which became tangible in His Son's earthly life. Moreover, he embraces the newborn babe of Bethlehem, Jesus, recognizing Him as a true Person, the God and Savior who became man on the holy night of His Nativity. Additionally, Father Matthew draws attention to Jesus' estrangement, sufferings, and sacrifice that was initiated at His

---

[1] *Wādī al-Rayyān* is a natural reserve and valley located 153 kms south of Cairo. This location was a suitable monastic dwelling due to its stillness. Cf. Otto Meinardus, "The Hermits of Wâdî Rayân," *Studia Orientalia Christiana* 11 (1966): 293-317.

birth until the moment He died on the Cross. Surely, a deep gaze from our side will let us realize that the manger, in which the infant Jesus was laid, paved the way that led Him to Calvary.

Alexandrian Theology at the Roots of Father Matthew's Nativity Letters

Since his initial monastic days, Father Matthew rooted himself in the Scriptures and the early patristic and ascetic writings of the Fathers. He tirelessly tapped into the well of the spiritual treasures of the Church, foundationally, the writings of the Desert Fathers—especially the *Letters* of Saint Antony the Great (251-356) and *The Spiritual Homilies* of Saint Macarius the Spiritbearer (300-391)—that nourished his day-to-day life. His theology springs from the Alexandrian tradition, specifically the writings of Saint Athanasius the Great (296-373) and Saint Cyril of Alexandria (375—444). These two Alexandrian patriarchs centered their theology on the mystery of the Lord's Incarnation, its enactment on humanity's salvation, and its Christology. In these writings, among others, as his theological building blocks, we find the roots of Father Matthew's teachings on the Nativity.

Moreover, the Nativity of Christ is at the heart of the Coptic Orthodox Church's liturgy and doctrine. If we look at the Coptic liturgy, we will realize from the first glance that the Incarnation is daily present in the Church's prayers, especially in the midnight praises and in its *Theotokias*.[2] As far as theology is concerned, the Alexandrian Church Fathers have perceived the Incarnation as the spring from which all the heavenly gifts flow onto us. The Incarnation is the instrument that God the Father used to reveal His love to us and to unite humans in Him through His Son Jesus Christ and the Holy Spirit.

Below, we highlight the strong correlation and reliance on Scripture, patristic and ascetic Fathers, and the liturgical sources that came to shape Father Matthew's theology on the Nativity. The Church

---

[2] *Theotokias* are a kind of hymn that uses typology and celebrate the mystery of God's incarnation. Many texts of the weekly *Theotokias* are influenced by the writings of Saint Cyril of Alexandria.

Fathers repeated many times the theological expression *for us* that they borrowed from the Scripture, especially from the epistles of the New Testament.[3] For instance, Saint Athanasius states that all Christ's works that took place during His life on earth were *for our sake*. In his *Contra Arianos,* he exclaimed:

> It will be well to listen to the blessed Peter... He writes then in his Epistle thus, 'Christ then having suffered for us in the flesh' (1 Pt. 4:1). Therefore also when He is said to hunger and thirst and to toil and not to know, and to sleep, and to weep, and to ask, and to flee, and to be born, and to deprecate the cup, and in a word to undergo

---

[3] This is clearly evident, for instance, in Saint Paul's statement, "For you know the grace of our Lord Jesus Christ, that though He was rich, yet *for your sakes* He became poor, that you through His poverty might become rich" (2 Cor. 8:9), and also "For He made Him who knew no sin to be sin *for us*, that we might become the righteousness of God in Him" (2 Cor. 5:21). As for Saint Peter, he repeats the same notion saying in his first epistle, "Therefore, since Christ suffered *for us* in the flesh, arm yourselves also with the same mind, for he who has suffered in the flesh has ceased from sin" (1 Pt. 4:1).

> all that belongs to the flesh, let it be said, as is congruous, in each case 'Christ then hungering and thirsting "for us in the flesh;"' and 'saying He did not know, and being buffeted, and toiling "for us in the flesh;"' and 'being exalted too, and born, and growing "in the flesh;"' and 'fearing and hiding "in the flesh;"' and 'saying, "If it be possible let this cup pass from Me," and being beaten, and receiving, "for us in the flesh;"' and in a word all such things 'for us in the flesh.' For on this account has the Apostle himself said, 'Christ then having suffered,' not in His Godhead, but 'for us in the flesh,' that these affections may be acknowledged as, not proper to the very Word by nature, but proper by nature to the very flesh.[4]

Another theological formula on which the Alexandrian Fathers insisted was the so-called 'exchange formula,' that "He [Christ] took what is

---

[4] Athanasius of Alexandria, *Orations Against the Arians*, 3:34. ET: John H. Newman (ed.), *Select Treatises of St. Athanasius*, Vol. I, (New York, NY: Longmans, Green and Company, 1903), 399.

ours and gave us what is His," which is the refrain of the Coptic Friday *Theotokia*. Similarly, we also read of the exchange formula in the writings of Saint Athanasius:

> As the Lord, putting on the body, became man, so we men are deified by the Word, as being taken to Him through His flesh, and henceforward inherit life everlasting.[5]

Saint Cyril of Alexandria follows Saint Athanasius in teaching that God took our nature so that we may be partakers of His divine life:

> Since He became like us (that is, a human being) in order that we might become like Him (I mean gods and sons), He receives our properties into Himself and He gives us His own in return.[6]

---

[5] Orations Against the Arians, 3:34. ET: Select Treatises of St. Athanasius, 400.

[6] Cyril of Alexandria, *Commentary on John* 20:17. ET: Joel C. Elowsky (ed.), *Commentary on John*, Ancient Christian Texts II, (Downers Grove, IL: IVP Academic, 2015), 363.

Saint Macarius the Great[7] reiterates in the same vein:

> The infinite, inaccessible, and uncreated God has assumed a body, and on account of His immense and ineffable kindness, if I may so say it, he diminished himself (cf. Phil. 2:6), lessening His inaccessible glory so as to be able to be united with His visible creatures, as with the souls of the saints and angels, so they can be made participators of divine life (cf. 2 Pt. 1:4).[8]

These three great Alexandrian Fathers of the Egyptian Church emphasize that Jesus took our flesh and humbled Himself so that we may appropriate the divine life by uniting ourselves with Him.

---

[7] A recent study with a foreword by prof. Sebastian Brock, *La balance du cœur, Un substrat égyptien aux homélies macariennes*, (Münster: LIT, 2021), offers evidence of the Egyptian origins of the macarian homilies and gives more probability to their attribution to Saint Macarius the Great.

[8] Macarius the Great, *Homily* 4:9, Collection II. ET: George A. Maloney (ed.), *Pseudo-Macarius, The Fifty Spiritual Homilies and the Great Letter*, (New York, NY: Paulist Press, 1992), 42.

Father Matthew the Poor and the Incarnation through his Letters

Father Matthew the Poor inherits the theological foundations of his Church and can be considered as a faithful disciple of Saint Athanasius, Saint Cyril and Saint Macarius. He elaborates on them, affirming in many of his homilies and writings[9] how we are partakers of Nativity.

This is especially evident in this epistolary. He underlines on many occasions that at the Incarnation we have been endowed with boundless gifts by God the Father through His Son Jesus Christ. Following the Alexandrian teachings, Father Matthew believes that all the salvific works of the incarnate God the Word were *for us men and for our salvation*, as we declare in the Nicene-Constantinopolitan Creed and as he expresses again and again in this epistolary.

Additionally, Father Matthew finds humanity at Bethlehem, for Christ's birth is our very same

---

[9] These works have been collected in an anthology called *'A'yād al-Ẓuhūr al-'Ilāhī* (The Theophanic Feasts) published by St Macarius Monastery Press.

birth, for as he writes:

> We are called to see Christ's birth in our own birth from God (*Letter 9*).

Echoing the famous exchange formula between Christ and humanity used by the Alexandrian Fathers as a benefit and outcome of the Incarnation, Father Matthew has never tired of emphasizing that Christ took our weakness to give us His strength; took our flesh in order to give us His Holy Spirit; assumed our poverty that we may be enriched by His richness, and also wore our nature to clothe us with His nature. For he articulated:

> Today, our nature has been donned with divinity, and divinity has been clothed with our nature (*Letter 1*).

The concealed reason behind this exchange was the Father's love for the whole world. Father Matthew was overwhelmed by this love as he eloquently expressed:

> Christ is the Son of love, and love can bring forth nothing except itself. Since the love of the

> heavenly Father is stored to be received only by spiritual, justified people, love born in the flesh has now become our portion to accept and embrace (*Letter 3*).

For Father Matthew Incarnation could be synthesized in one very simple, yet profound sentence:

> Love took flesh; sacrifice became a body. When the Father's love for sinners united with the Son's love for the Father, Christ was born (*Letter 6*).

Although most of the letters were addressed to monks, they continue as a source of spiritual inspiration for all readers. While it is undeniable that this collection has a peculiar monastic flavor, since Father Matthew does not take off his monastic cloak when talking about the spiritual dimensions of the Incarnation, yet they echo and augment the Christian and salvific reality of Christ's birth for the sake of humanity due to the Father's love. Although monasticism is considered a way of the Cross after which all monks are called 'Cross-bearers,' self-denial is nonetheless a general calling for all Christians. The author reads the Incarnation in light of the Cross, teaching that there is only one true legitimate path to obtain the blessings of Nativity—Calvary with all its sufferings. Thus, he underscores that:

> Today, you have begun upon the path leading to Calvary that starts from a manger. Bow down your heads, you who are chosen by God, that you may enter the manger of beasts. It is in there that your salvation lies (*Letter 14*).

Therefore, we can only comprehend the Nativity in the shadow of the Cross, since the path leading to Calvary starts at the manger.

As a contemporary desert father, Father Matthew perceives Christ's estrangement at the Nativity as a source of inspiration. Christ came to us as a stranger and we must follow His footsteps. He even goes to the point of defining Nativity as "the feast of estrangement" when he exclaimed that

> the Nativity is the feast of estrangement and sojourning (*Letter 12*).

It is appropriate to conclude with a synthesis of

Father Matthew's theology of the Nativity from his disciple, the late abbot of Saint Macarius' Monastery, Bishop Epiphanius (1954—2018). He wrote these few words as a foreword to the Italian translation of an anthology of Father Matthew's texts on the Incarnation:

> It is no longer a question of simply celebrating the Lord's birth, but of our union with him and our birth in him. This is how we began to understand and become aware that the mystery of the Incarnation and the virginal birth are realities that concern us first, and not events that concern the Lord Jesus regardless of us.[10]

Glimpses of Father Matthew the Poor's Biography

Born Yūsuf Iskandar in Banhā, Egypt, on September 20, 1919, from a poor family, Father Matthew joined the Faculty of Pharmacy in 1939. Upon graduating, he labored as a pharmacist and quickly became successful, which secured him a bright future. The young pharmacist became

---

[10] Matta el Meskin, *L'umanità di Dio*, ed. by Markos el Makari (Magnano, Italy: Qiqajon 2016):6.

famous for his generosity with the needy and for his love and empathy to everyone with no conditions or discrimination. But despite his professional success, he counted all as a loss to gain Christ as Saint Paul taught (cf. Phil. 3:7).

On August 15, 1948, Yūsuf joined the Monastery of Saint Samuel the Confessor in Mount Qalamūn, 175 kms south of Cairo—one of the most remote and isolated Egyptian monasteries at that time. Due to his fragile health, the young monk struggled for three years to cope with the harsh living conditions of the monastery. After Father Matthew's health deteriorated, his spiritual father, the hermit Mīnā al-Barāmūsī (later Pope Kyrillos VI, 1902-1971), advised Father Matthew to go and visit the Monastery of Virgin Mary known as al-Suryān located in the Scetis Desert (Wādī al-Naṭrūn), 123 kms north of Cairo. There, he was ordained as a priest against his will and became the confessor for many of the young, educated monks of that generation. Soon after, Father Matthew and his disciples were forced to leave this monastery taking residence in the caves of *Wādī al-*

Rayyān from 1960 to 1969. Despite the caves' harshness, they were a great blessing for Father Matthew and for his small community. Prior to this period, he had penned his masterpiece on the Church *al-Kanīsa al-Ḫālida* (The Church Immortal),[11] some of his formative articles on the Holy Spirit, *Guidelines for Prayer,*[12] and others.

In 1969, after nine years living as hermits, the small community was invited by pope Kyrillos VI to move to their final settlement at the Monastery of Saint Macarius the Great in the Scetis Desert. This monastery was in ruins and inhabited by six elderly and sick monks. Under the guidance of Father Matthew, both a monastic revival and architectural restorations occurred in the monastery.

By virtue of his openness and love for the mystical Body of Christ, Father Matthew was a great

---

[11] St Macarius Press is currently working on a new series that will include this work in an anthology of Father Matthew the Poor's writings on Ecclesiology and Church Unity.

[12] See the expanded and revised version: Matthew the Poor, *Guidelines for Prayer* (Wādī al-Nāṭrūn, Egypt: St Macarius Press, 2021).

advocate of unity and communion between churches. Although he did not travel around the world nor was he invited to conferences or even attended any ecumenical talks, Father Matthew was on every occasion encouraging and supporting the Church unity movement. Some of the Christian Churches' prominent figures, like the Archbishop George Cary of Canterbury (b. 1935), Bishop Geoffrey Rowell of Europe (1943-2017), dom Emmanuel Lanne (1923-2010), and Archpriest Alexander Schmemann (1921-1983), visited him at the monastery.

Father Matthew became a prolific writer and penned almost 180 books (in addition to countless articles) still circulating in Egypt, the Middle East, and many parts of the world. His translated works assisted spreading his voice—which encompasses his Alexandrian ascetic-patristic heritage—all over the world. Father Matthew, however, constantly pointed out that he was not a creative writer but merely a transmitter of the Alexandrian heritage received and acquired through his own experience.

At the age of 86, on June 8, 2006, Father Matthew rested in the Lord, leaving behind an exceptional spiritual legacy that still nourishes many Christians around the whole world.

Paope 20, 1738 / October 30, 2021
Feast of St. John Kolobos

Editorial Notes

All the letters (except one) are taken from *Rasā'il Al-Qummuṣ Mattā Al-Miskīn* (Wādī Al-Naṭrūn, Egypt: Monastery of Saint Macarius 2007), and, unlike the Arabic anthology, they have been arranged according to the affinity of the subject rather than chronologically. Father Mattew the Poor originally penned these letters as separate letters and he did not intend to deliver one whole message. On the contrary, they were composed for different persons with dissimilar needs and backgrounds. Moreover, since the letters were personal, the addressees are kept confidential here. Most of the letters were sent to the monks dwelling in the caves of *Wādī al-Rayyān*, between 1967 and 1969.

All the quotations are taken from New King James Version, unless specifically noted otherwise and all footnotes are the translator's.

Almost all the letters are signed *Al-Qummuṣ Mattā Al-Miskīn* (Hegumen Matthew the Poor).

The signature is omitted in the translated texts.

Letter 1, "Rejoice for the Divine Gift we are Given," corresponds to letter 36 of the Arabic collection, *Naḥnu Šurakā' Fī Al-'Ahd Al-Ğadīd Ka-Nā'ilīn Al-'Aṭiyya* (We are Partakers of the New Covenant as Receivers of a Gift, 145–146).

Letter 2, "Why Don't we Rejoice?", corresponds to letter 23 of the Arabic collection, *Limāḏā Lā Yafraḥ Al-'Insān* (Why does Man not Rejoice?, 112–113).

Letter 3, "Christ, God's Free Gift to Humanity," corresponds to letter 30 of the Arabic collection, *Māḏa 'A'ṭānā Al-Masīḥ Wa-Māḏa Lam Yu'ṭinā?* (What Did Christ Give us and What he Did not?, 130–131).

Letter 4, "My Power is made Perfect in Weakness," corresponds to letter 35 of the Arabic collection, *Ḍu'f Al-Ṭufūla Wa-Quwwat Allāh* (Childhood's Weakness and God's Power, 143–144).

Letter 5, "Christ, Our True Life," corresponds to letter 37 of the Arabic collection, *Bad' Ḥayātinā Al-Ḥaqīqiyya Wa-l-'Abadiyya* (The Beginning of our True and Eternal Life, 147–148).

Letter 6, "Love Took Flesh", corresponds to

letter 38 of the Arabic collection, *'Īd Bākūrat Ṯamar Al-Bašariyya* (The Feast of Humanity's First Fruit, 149-150).

Letter 7, "The Gift of Christ's Humility," corresponds to letter 39 of the Arabic collection, *'Aṭā' Al-Ḥubb Wa-Hibat Al-Ittiḍā' Fī Al-Masīḥ* (The Gift of Love and Humility in Christ, 151-152).

Letter 8, "Today, Joy is our Strength", corresponds to letter 40 of the Arabic collection, *Mīlād Ibn Allāh Bi-l-Ğasad 'A'ṭānā Ḥaqq Al-Mīlād Bi-l-Rūḥ* (The Son of God's Birth in the Flesh Gave us the Right to Be Born in the Spirit, 153-154).

Letter 9, "The Birth of Christ is Our Birth," corresponds to letter 31 of the Arabic collection, *Mīlād Al-Masīḥ Wa-Mīlādunā Naḥnu Min Allāh* (Christ's Birth and Our Birth from God, 133-136).

Letter 10, "He Alone Suffices," corresponds to letter 32 of the Arabic collection, *Du'īnā Li-'An Nakūn Fī Ṭa'at Ṭufūlat Al-Masīḥ* (We Have Been Called to Be Obedient as the Christ Child, 137-138).

Letter 11, "Our Eucharistic Bread is Born Today in Bethlehem," corresponds to letter 33 of the Arabic collection, *Al-Yawm Wulida Qurbānunā Fī*

Bayt Laḥm (Today, Our Offering Was Born in Bethlehem, 139-140).

Letter 12, "Nativity as the Feast of Estrangement," corresponds to letter 75 of the Arabic collection, *'Īd Al-Mīlād Huwa 'Īd Al-Ġurba* (The Feast of Nativity is a Feast of Estrangement, 275-278).

Letter 13, "Glory in Poverty", corresponds to letter 79 of the Arabic collection, *Al-Bišāra Al-Mufriḥa* (The Good Tidings, 302-306).

Letter 14, "From the Manger to Calvary," corresponds to letter 2 of the Arabic collection, *Tawǧīhāt Rahbāniyya 2* (Monastic Guidelines 2, 26-30).

Letter 15, "The Joy that Christ Came to Bring on Earth," is an unpublished text, both in Arabic and in any translation.

1

Rejoice for the Divine Gift we are Given

Dear Father,

Peace from God to your spirit, my beloved!

I would like to send you my greetings for Nativity. For the first time after his fall, man heard a voice from Heaven that comforted his heart and called him to peace and joy. Blessed is that day, for it became a day of comfort for humankind and power of joy that is always able to turn all our sorrows into hope.

The reader of the books of prophecies in the Old Testament is shocked to find them full of woes, sorrows, and threats that the prophets poured one after another over all nations and peoples—"The oracle concerning… the oracle concerning… the oracle concerning…" (cf. Jer. 23). One's heart almost stops in terror at the overabundant fearful threats from Heaven.

However, thank God Almighty who has done away with the age of wrath and woe, and opened a new era in the destiny of all nations and peoples on the day when Christ was born, "a light to bring revelation to the Gentiles, and the glory of Your people Israel" (Luke 2:32).

How beautiful Isaiah is, and how wonderful is his consoling voice, "Comfort, yes, comfort My people!" (Isa. 40:1). The psalmist cries out saying, "This is the day that the Lord has made; let us rejoice and be glad in it!" (Ps. 117:24). For it is a day of salvation freely given, a day of redemption from God, a day of treaty issued by one party who is God alone. Humankind plays no part in it except by offering the pure body of the Virgin to God to use as a tabernacle to dwell in, that He might fulfill His promise with His own arm.

We are actual partakers in the new covenant, not as superintendent agents, but receivers of a gift. How generous is this communion! How easy is our role! For the blood that was shed is our own—scarlet red and flaming. Yet, the power latent within it is divine and of an extraordinary action and efficacy. It is a body and blood that bears our own weakness, and alongside it, the power of our salvation.

Look up to Bethlehem and ponder for the born Babe is your own Son and Lord. He bears your nature and it is He who sanctifies and redeems it.

Today our nature has been donned with divinity, and divinity has been clothed with our nature.

Today weakness has been turned into strength, and sin has dwindled to be replaced by eternal righteousness.

Farewell!

2

Why don't we Rejoice?

Dear Father,

May the peace of God which surpasses all understanding be with your beloved soul and may His peace abound to be a fruitful tree which flowers in springtime, having received by the warmth of the Holy Spirit the ability to bear the fruit of grace and offer nourishment for every living soul. May God bless him who plants and him who waters, and glorify the skillful hand that allows our nature to share God's own divine nature.

The time has come. "Let your servant depart in peace" (Luke 2:31). Simeon the Elder rejoices because Christ has been born in a place for beasts. The low point is lifted up to God's Heaven of Heavens; the crooked ways have been made straight by the mere touch of the Spirit; the obstacles have been removed in the silence of the night; and the daylight of salvation has shined upon the way, paving it upon the arid land of despondent hearts.

Why then should we not rejoice? Why should the angels not exult? Peace has just been planted in the very core of the earth. The joy of the Spirit has suddenly sprung forth amidst the thorns of sorrows. Those who do not wish to believe what is written, let them come to us to believe what is seen. Let them place the finger of doubt on the wound of sin; let them feel the pulses of grace instead of the stirrings of sin and hear God's heart beating beneath the sound of their own amazement.

After all that, those who do not wish to believe, let them take a look around, for the very stones are about to cry out, a cry that would deafen the ears… Today, there has emerged from the silence of the Church a voice crying that the time has come for the travail of childbirth. Christ is about to be formed in the hearts of many. A whole nation may be born in one day (cf. Is. 66:8). Instead of the silence of fourteen centuries, the barren will cry out through the mouths of countless children. The light of the Holy Spirit will dawn and be poured out profusely on every oppressed or crushed person, in place of the darkness that guilty hands have embraced throughout countless generations. Faith will cover the earth in readiness for the One who is to come, that Christ may find His heart's desire.

Trim your lamp, O wise people! (cf. Matt. 25:1-13). Let the light of your poverty and contrition shine so that everyone in the house may know that we look forward to a better city whose foundations are built by God (cf. Heb. 11:10). Let your eyes always look upwards to where the happy end lies and where your portion is being prepared for you. Do not become entangled in the unfruitful works of darkness, but rather be filled with peace through prayer and spiritual work.

Resort to find shelter in God's wings in evil times; He will carry you away. Have no anxiety about anything, but in everything, let your prayers be known to God, who seals with His faithful promises every work done sincerely in His name.

Peace, Peace, Peace!

3

Christ, God's Free Gift to Humanity

Dear Beloved Brethren,

You are a little church adorned with the Holy Spirit, a happy flock enjoying its meek Shepherd who Himself is like a lamb. I would like to bring you the breeze of Bethlehem of Judea where Christ was born. According to our faith and liturgy, it is as if His birth has only occurred yesterday, even today or this very moment, for the holy liturgy is retrospective in its focus. In other words, it breathes life into the past and makes it a present reality to be lived out here and now, just like yesterday, and to the end of all ages. For when we gaze at the little Babe, we see the perfect God with a full stature in relation to existence, time, and being, for as it is said, "All things were made through

Him, and without Him, nothing was made that was made" (John 1:3).

Tonight, we celebrate Nativity, but our feast extends to embrace all days, and maybe the whole history of humankind forever.

Celebrating Nativity transcends events, outward appearances, places, and persons by reaching out to the heart of divine will, that is, the will of the Father from whom Christ directly descended. Within that will we find the spring of true love that gushed forth on Nativity Day. Ever since that time, it has been incessantly poured out into our hearts. Christ's birth is the climax of the revelation of the Father's will of love for us, we who had been rejected for so long. We were children of wrath, enslaved to iniquity and dwelling in darkness. Only now have we become children of light and love.

Brethren, Christ is the Son of love, and love can bring forth nothing except itself. Since the love of the Heavenly Father is stored to be received only by spiritual, justified people, love born in the flesh has now become our portion to accept and embrace. Once we manage to grasp love in its incarnate form and own it, never letting it go of our hands, we shall become one with that love in its spiritual form. It is only then that the Father's love may become palpable to us, for he who loves the Son inevitably also loves the Father.

Christ's love is a commodity exhibited for sale for a very low price in the world's market, which teems with many other kinds of love. Many are those who overlook that commodity, finding nothing in it that appeals to their senses. They prefer pleasure, covetousness, love of a partner, son, daughter, or money, fame or power, etc. They thus slight Christ's love and fail to honor the Father's will manifest in that love. Such people are those described as spurning the Spirit of grace and profaning the blood by which they have been sanctified, counting it on equal terms with the rest of this world's profanities that draw their attention. In their hunt for lust, possession, and false glory, they trample underfoot the Son of God (cf. Heb. 10:29).

As for those who have responded to God's

offering—cheap and despised as it is in the eyes of the world—they honor His Son and set His love as their only goal. They willingly pay the price, not just out of their pockets, honor, or bodies but also from their life. They relish any forfeiture and downplay every insult in return for Christ's love, gratuitous as it is, asking nothing in return. Such people obtain from God permission to be counted as God's children. For, having loved the Son of God, they are qualified to resemble Him in the sight of His Father. Scripture confirms that the Son has been given the power to divide His inheritance among His beloved, that is, to divide His Kingdom, glory, and His Father's love for Him (cf. John 17:26).

Brethren, see what gift the Father has given us today! He did not give us Christ to make something for our advantage in this world. Nor did He send Him on His behalf to deliver a message of comfort or encouragement to us in our difficult journey across this world. Yet, the Father has given us the person of Christ along with everything that belongs to Christ. Namely, His

Kingdom, His glory, His love, and even His life with His Father.

Among what least belongs to Christ is His relationship with this age, along with its princes and prelates. They are counted as masters over people, reigning over them with the credentials of this world. This does not count among the gifts given to us by the Father through Christ. For this reason, anyone who claims such credentials must deny Christ.

Brethren, see how and why Christ has been born in a manger for animals. He could not even find a proper swaddle to wrap Himself in and therefore had recourse to old rags. Isn't this one of the most genuine characteristics of Christ? If we acquire this godsend tonight, it would result in nothing short of a new annunciation, the annunciation of the true birth of our souls.

I would also like to skip ahead and say, look at Christ who was slapped by a slave of the high priest and could not find a single person to plead His case. He, therefore, begged the slave to tell Him why he struck Him. Isn't that a very special feature of Christ? If we act likewise today, would not that be a manifestation of the cross to which we have attained?

Finally, glory be to the Father who has given us Christ along with all that belongs to Him.

Glory be to the Son who has apportioned us His inheritance.

Glory be to the Holy Spirit who has set our hearts aflame with the love of Christ.

Amen!

4

"My Power is made Perfect in Weakness"

Dear Father,

Peace from God to your spirit, my beloved!

Nativity greetings mixed with heavenly joy in which the voices of singing people cannot be distinguished from those of angels. Both are absorbed by the same vision in which God's absolute fatherly love that is full of extraordinary compassion and humility was incarnate in Jesus as an eternal gift to the children of man. In Him are all the wisdom and dispensation of God revealed. Therefore, Christ has become the bearer of the Father's glory and the recipient of all worship to God. In Christ, the ultimate aim of creation is fulfilled, as in Him everything had its beginning (cf. John 1:3).

Jesus began His life on earth as a helpless Babe, but ended it with the Resurrection from the dead in all power. This was to prove that He is truly the Alpha and Omega, the beginning and the end. We, therefore, find in Him strength in our extreme weakness, and uttermost weakness in our strength; for He bears both strength and humility. Consequently, Christ covers the frailties of those who have put Him on and exposes those who rely on their own abilities.

King Herod wanted to kill the baby Jesus; for he thought the helplessness of infancy as a good occasion to wield his foolish sword. However, God's weakness can never lie within the reach of the foolish or oppressive arm of man, for the weakness of God is stronger than men. As for Satan, he was vanquished forever through the Cross.

We, as humans, are weak, regardless of however powerful, tyrannical, or heavy-handed we may be or even how saintly, righteous or pious we may be! But true power that remains forever and from which springs all victory derives from Christ alone through free grace. This is only achievable when we believe in the veracity of our weakness. We must lose all hope in relying on our power or artificial means of success through our mind, money, or guile. Only then can we draw upon Christ's limitless power that comes forth from His divinity.

Thank God that He has led us to the source of human weakness that we may face ourselves in reality, realize our nothingness and be sure of God's power. Nothing remains but to accept our weakness in order to receive God's power.

Farewell!

5

Christ, Our True Life

Dear Father,

Peace from God to your spirit, my beloved!

I send your beloved soul greetings for the Nativity, the feast with which we begin our new year,[1] the acceptable year of the Lord (cf. Isa. 61:2). Or rather, we begin our life in God and eternal salvation, a life that the Scripture speaks of as another life that bears spiritual features. Such features are not subject to the influences of this age. Such a life does not draw upon the flesh for happiness, for, as it is written in the gospel of John, "Destroy this temple, and in three days I will raise it up" (John 2:19), and "I do not receive honor from

---

[1] The Coptic Orthodox Church celebrates the feast of the Nativity relatively close to the new year, on January 7th.

men" (John 5:41).

Although Christ lived out His life on earth in a body that had all the faculties of bodily existence and was subject to all temporal influences, He nonetheless proved, by His Resurrection, to have been neither of nor for the flesh. It was a divine life that appeared in the flesh, as written "the eternal life which was with the Father and was manifested to us… which we have seen with our eyes… our hands have handled" (1 John 1:2).

This divine mystery of multifold power and depth began simply in Bethlehem as if it were natural. Yet, its wonder and miracle were revealed on the day of the Baptism in the Jordan River, as it became surely known that the Babe born in Bethlehem was the incarnated, eternal Life that became flesh. This took place according to the good pleasure of the Father in the hypostasis of the Son who became man. For this reason, the wise early Church used to celebrate Nativity and Epiphany on the same day since Epiphany was considered the manifestation of the eternal birth that has been revealed in the bodily birth of Christ, so much so that we cannot possibly separate the one from the other.

In exactly the same pattern, we begin our divine life, which is true and eternal life, with baptism. In baptism we receive the Spirit of Christ, that is, the Spirit of the Son, or, to be more precise, the Spirit of the Father that proceeds from Him in the Son (cf. John 15:26). He gives birth to us once again, anew (cf. Rom. 6:4). Or rather, He gives birth to us anew from God. Eternal life thus begins to flow and grow mystically deep inside us. Henceforth, we begin to live out an eternal life with Christ in God that transcends all the influences of this age along with all the defects and infirmities of the flesh.

This increases the lucidity and closeness of our eternal life to its divine essence, which is able to swallow up death and corruption entirely. Eventually, the spiritual essence of our life will become transfigured in all its splendor and divine perfection. Only then will every tongue shout with joy for God's great mercy in Christ, which has made up for all our weakness, suffering, or tears and replaced them with joy, jubilation, comfort, and happiness.

Farewell!

6

Love took Flesh

Dear Father,

Peace from God to your spirit, my beloved!

I send you Nativity greetings, gentle like a breeze in which the voice of the Fatherly love was heard in Bethlehem harmonically chanted by the angels. What a refreshing and lifegiving voice it was that quickened the dead, despondent humanity! The voice was not a message but a body in which all the mercies of God were revealed. The body carried His compassion and forgiveness for all the sins that He had forbore for so long in patience and long-suffering beyond comprehension. Such was the baby Jesus lying in a manger which was the pledge of the Cross that took place in its due time. Such is Jesus, who was born to die for us. Love took flesh; sacrifice became a body. When the Father's love for sinners united with the Son's love for the Father, Christ was born.

Today, after the sterility of spirit that had befallen our two ancestors, humanity has become fertile. Today has been born to humanity a Son who is called an everlasting God (cf. Isa 9:6). Today, we celebrate the birth of the first-fruit of humanity, the first-born among many brethren (cf. Rom. 8:29), the head of the spiritual Church that fills Heaven. He is the sole Mediator between us and the Father, for He is our brother and the Son of God at one and the same time. He is able in all veracity, aptness, and worthiness to intercede for any guilt or weakness on our part; for He has deigned to bear all of our sin before the Father and the angels, and to accept in its stead reproach and punishment. After purifying our nature, He donned us with His pure body that we might appear in it before the Father—blameless and without blemish.

So, blessed is that day among all the days of humanity, the day on which we handed over our body to the Holy Spirit through the Virgin so that Christ could take it on our behalf, turn it into His own, and appear in it before the Father to reconcile everyone in that body to Himself. Blessed are those who bear within themselves the Spirit of Christ in faith, for they will not appear anymore henceforth in their own dead, corrupt body before the Father but will be offered Christ's body that they may appear in it, and so receive grace. Upon them, God's glory will come.

Farewell!

7

The Gift of Christ's Humility

Dear Father,

Peace from God to your spirit, my beloved!

I would like to send you Nativity greetings filled with love and humility, both of which were incarnated at the moment of the Nativity as two new powers injected into our world, present in our own nature once accepted willingly.

Blessed is the Father who revealed His love to us, manifesting His humility in the person of Jesus Christ. For it is not only through revelation that He made known to us the mystery He cherished for us in His heart, but also through the sending of His only beloved Son. The Lord Jesus was sent not at best to reveal personally His Father's love towards us, nor only to reveal the mystery of His humility which He accepted in order to complete our own salvation, but also to offer us the self-same love of the Father in an incarnate and tangible form—to offer us the mystery of His humility as a power that resides in us and totally guarantees our salvation.

The offering of love and the gift of humility in Christ cannot be recognized without Him nor can they be obtained apart from one another in His living person, not even for a single moment nor a twinkling of an eye. For the love that is offered to us by Christ is the Fatherly Spirit poured into Him, and the humility that Christ offers us is His insulted, flogged, wounded, dead-yet-alive body.

What can we see in Bethlehem except pure love swaddled in amazing humility, and a mother who, rapt in the Spirit, can only feel in her pangs of birth the angels ascending and descending between Heaven and earth, while her worn-out body lays on the straw of a manger? The Babe is her very son who bears all the human qualities along with human nature. Yet, He is the self-same eternal Son who rests in the bosom of the Father (cf. John

1:18). He appeared in the flesh to converge within Himself all that belongs to the Father and humankind.

What do we see in Bethlehem today besides a divine presence whose content is love, whose means is humility, and whose end is salvation? We are the object of that love, our nature is the instrument through which that humility is revealed, and our sin, humiliation, and poverty are the arena by which the action of salvation takes place.

Today we are the object of Bethlehem.

We celebrate the feast of the Fatherly love, announce the beatitude of our poor human nature that has become a tabernacle for the divinity, and exult in the salvation which has become ours.

Farewell!

8

Today, Joy is our Strength

Dear Father,

Peace from God to your spirit, my beloved!

I send you greetings for Nativity, the first feast of the Church in which she celebrates the birth of her Bridegroom. On this day, God visited the church of the wilderness (the Old Covenant), the barren that travailed with the pangs and wailings of the prophets, not giving birth except to a contentious people that died in the wilderness, whose remnant went corrupt.

Today, however, the promise is fulfilled in the birth of the Church of the righteous, God's own possession. The mystery of Bethlehem is revealed to us through baptism, and the birth of the Son of God in the flesh has given us the right to be born in the Spirit. Today, therefore, is the feast of the Church. It is the mystery of her baptism, and the power in which she stands and endures.

In its Greek etymology, the word *Church ekklēsia* means "those called to appear," and comes from the verb *ekkaléō*. That is to say, they are called to move from the invisible to the visible, just as the Son of God was called to appear from the invisible to the visible to proclaim the love of the Father. The Church then derives its name and being from the divine Nativity Day on which God's saving love appeared to all people (cf. Tit. 2:11).

Today, we are called to appear publicly with joy together with good tidings, just as the heavenly Church was represented in the choirs of angels and appeared to the children of Adam. We now openly release our previously suppressed voices within our hearts in public praises amidst the Church, as we declare our joy to the angels as a response and reaction to their good news. They once revealed to us the tidings of Nativity and we now declare our response reiterating these tidings daily and forever.

Yet it is not only through our voices and tongues that the Church announces the good tidings, or speaks out or preaches, but also through the lives of her pious members and worshipers—the living and the dead. The Church can present them as a sign of her response to the love of God declared in a manger. She can also present them as a humble model that succeeded to the humility of Him who is swaddled in rags.

Today, joy is our strength, and good pleasure is our nourishment.

Farewell!

9

The Birth of Christ is Our Birth

Dear Fathers of *Wādī al-Rayyān*,[1]

Peace from God and grace and blessing in Christ, the Redeemer and Savior of your souls!

Just as ever since we have sinned against God, the world had been looking forward to receiving the birth of Christ, so every one of us now looks forward to receiving Christ every time he or she sins against God. Christ came to rectify our course of life permanently and perpetually toward God. We always commit sins against God, but Christ is now ever-present to rectify our transgression. Christ is ever ready to restore the rectitude of the relationship that binds us to God, substantiate the feeling of renewal, and secure the ultimate aim of

[1] See footnote 1, page 9.

our existence. God actualizes all this by proving His divine existence within the very depths of our consciousness.

However, just as the world was growing in its readiness to receive the birth of Christ, it was also growing in its lack of readiness to believe in Him. This is so because the world contained and still contains intrinsic fundamental powers that defy God, which are the powers represented by the Prince of this world. It is those powers that hold sway over our passions and egotistic ambitions. They suggest to our mind to aspire to dissoluteness and the lust for power. They also beguile us to exist independently of God, far from His commandments and statutes.

Within every one of us, even when we grow in our submission to God and faith, there remain in us wrong inclinations and whims of egoistic ambitions growing alongside the passage of time and the activity of the world. We may yield to the enticement of aspiring to sinful freedom and an impure lifestyle away from the holy commandments of God. However, the birth of Christ into the world puts a limit to the tyranny of our cunningness. Now there exists Him who reproaches the world for its waywardness and overwhelming sway. Likewise, our birth in Christ sets a limit to the tyranny and arrogance of our passions and selfish ambition. It tames our wild nature and pricks our conscience unrelentingly for every word or deed that is in discord with the new life the Holy Spirit lavishes bountifully upon us as men and women of God.

Christ was not born into the world to stay in the world, for He is not originally of the world (cf. John 8:23). He was born to the world that the world might exist in Him. Therefore, we cannot see Christ in the world or the company of the world, which means that it is of no use fooling ourselves by attempting to recognize Him, feel Him, submit to Him, or even believe in Him while we live in the realm of this world with its thoughts, pleasures, ambitions, getting along with the world, currying its favor and seeking its affection. However, the moment we exit the realm of this world and become unshackled from its thoughts, pleasures, and ambitions, the moment we sacrifice its affection and favor and head directly toward God with our innermost self, we will immediately find Christ, recognizing Him and feeling His presence in an exceptional fashion. This is usually bolstered by a transcendent power and by gifts that overflow in abundance, making up for any loss exacted upon us by the world in return for our defiance of it.

When we are initiated into the realm of Christ, we discover the new world for which Christ is born to reign over from His throne forever. This new world is termed "The Kingdom of God." It is the world of the justified humanity which is subject to God; the world of saints and the spirits of angels; the world of the living Church and the mystical Body; the world of eternal light.

So, to everyone who believes in Christ and is baptized in His name, Christ is not revealed as born far away from him or her, in Bethlehem, nor is He revealed as merely born in one's heart. If we envisage it, this would turn the substance of true revelation into a merely historical one, which is only an image of the truth. The true mystical revelation of Christ's birth in relation to us only occurs precisely when we are born to God in Christ. So, through faith and the mystical, spiritual baptism in Christ, we receive the mystery of divine birth from God. Scripture expresses it this way:

> But as many as received Him, to them He gave the right to become children of God, to those who believe in His name: who were born, not of blood, nor of the will of the flesh, nor of the will of man, but of God (John 1:12-13).

Therefore, we are called to see Christ's birth in our own birth from God, a birth actualized by divine power which does not depend on any power on our part, but on the power of faith working through love. It is not affected by any sin inherited through the flesh but transcends every sin by washing it with the blood of Christ which is extraordinary in its mercy, kindness, and compassion for our weakness.

For this reason, everyone who lives out his or her new birth in Christ lives and sees the heavenly

Bethlehem as the angels perceive. Henceforth, he will never stop praising God's glory in the highest day and night, nor will he ever cease to delve deep into the peace of Christ on earth, nor to discern God's joy amidst the tribulations of this age.

Brethren, we are bonded together on this occasion by the fact that one of the most amazing mysteries of Christ has been conveyed to us… The Spirit of Christ has clothed us with the garbs of love and lavished the grace of humility upon our poverty, weakness, and humiliation. He then fused our hearts together into one, that we may rejoice together, grieve together, fall ill together, and give thanks together. We, therefore, step forward to petition God to sanctify our unity, love, misery, joy, grief, illness, and thanksgiving, and turn them into a living sacrifice, holy and acceptable to Him, for the sake of the love and honor due to His blessed and great name.

10

He alone Suffices

Dear Father,

Peace from God to your beloved soul!

I send to your beloved person greetings on the occasion of the Nativity, the feast of the ever-renewable hope of humankind. No matter how darkness or stagnation may envelop humanity, the Nativity comes with its powerful light to illumine the heart of every one of us. Christ's birth comes with the overwhelming power to disperse every dimness or doubt and it is able to spread the warmth of its joy over cold hearts, turning such coldness into a power that moves the whole world.

Humanity, represented in Israel, no less than the Gentiles, had been drudging under the yoke of death and suffering from the coldness of spiritual darkness as it lay in the shadows of nothingness until the day Christ dawned upon humanity through the angels announcing the good tidings. The children of Israel, who were called—the children of the Kingdom, the sons of the Light, the holders of the keys of knowledge, the sages of Israel erudite in God's Kingdom, the sons of the prophets, the custodians of the promises, the legislators of virtue and the law of righteousness—all of them lay in the darkness of death and ignorance. They were all consigned to disobedience, which had been the case that God might show that there is no kingdom, light, knowledge, wisdom, learning, hope in a promise, or value of legislation, virtue, law, or righteousness apart from Christ.

What joy, therefore, do we have today in Christ! He alone suffices. God has declared that He is our righteousness, holiness, and redemption (cf. 1 Cor. 1:30). What then is there beyond Christ? It is He in whom all the treasures of wisdom and knowledge are hidden (cf. Col. 2:3). When we accept Him and provide Him room in our hearts, that becomes like a treasure of goodness out of which good things flow. Those hearts even become a source of grace that pours out the Holy Spirit with all His knowledge, understanding, reverence, poise, and love.

Christ has become a law in Himself, yet not inscribed in letters, but in living action that holds sway over our thought, will, acts, and whole life. Eventually, all these end up according to His holy will, which works out our salvation from this age. This takes place when we receive Him and accept His will with all surrendering and contentment.

A lovely image of Christ's obedience to the Father is presented in His infancy; an infancy that surrendered to God's hand amid an ocean of human wickedness. Yet, this infancy was kept safe from any harm in all wisdom and insight.

We are thus called, under the protection of the Father's providence, to live in the obedience of such infancy that we may be qualified for His wisdom. This is our only option if we are to stand firm in His eternal Kingdom and revel in the joy of His will. Farewell!

11

Our Eucharistic Bread is Born in Bethlehem Today

Dear Father,

Peace from God to your beloved soul!

I would like to send you Nativity greetings that diffuse the pleasant odor of an oblation which is the most sacred and pure oblation that man has ever known. Today, the altar of the showbread has been annulled. Instead of the warm bread that the priest presented on the altar, which turned cold quickly and if neglected for a moment would have rotted, today the Body that ignites God's fire into cold hearts has been born. The Body turns our cold hearts into a furnace of love that does not cease to burn until it has consumed every sin in man. This Bread is aflame with the divinity that has conquered the coldness of death, raising the body back to life, and continues to raise whomever hears Christ's voice from the grave.

Today, our Eucharistic bread is born in Bethlehem, the living Bread which has descended from Heaven and was sealed by God. Everyone who eats it is impressed with the seal of the Spirit, and so becomes a living sacrifice and an acceptable offering.

In the former days, the showbread was only eaten by those who held priestly qualifications. Yet, now Christ has become a common food for everybody for He is able to make everyone a priest to the living God. Therefore, the Christ's oblation has become a new unction, a horn of oil that anoints one's heart with joy, and coronates our spirit with a crown bearing the words, "Holy to the Lord."

Today, the Holy Spirit has fashioned out of Mary "a batch of dough of humanity." [1] He

---

[1] In a passage from the holy annual Coptic Psalmody, we chant: "Oh what a great prodigy! She who was taken from the rib of Adam's side, to be molded as a woman, gave all

sanctified her and cut from her a piece of dough that the Son singled out as His own, has unified with His divinity, and has handed over to the children of sinners to raise as an offering on their behalf, despite them, on the Cross. Mary the wise cherished the secret of this Bread until the day of its offering arrived. Just before the appointed time, she said to Him, "Reveal Yourself!" (cf. John 2).

Today, we gather around the manger to rejoice over the Bread of our life (cf. John 6:48). He is the strength of our priesthood through which we have obtained boldness and confidence of access to God's throne.

Farewell!

---

humanity's batch of dough in all perfection to God the Creator and Word of the Father" (*sixth stanza of the Thursday Theotokia*). Here is one of the many paradoxes of the Incarnation on which the Coptic hymnology and Father Matthew the Poor ruminate: she who is the new Eve, Mary, whose body God had taken from Adam's rib, is now the one who offers the new Adam, God himself, a human body, equal to ours in everything, except for sin, in which to be incarnate.

12

NATIVITY AS THE FEAST OF ESTRANGEMENT

Dear Beloved,

Just as mercy and truth have met together and righteousness and peace have kissed each other (cf. Ps. 84:10) in the person of the Lord Jesus, who shone upon us from the earth and who descended to us from Heaven, my soul desires to encounter your soul, my beloved.

Let us sing together with ease and simplicity what the angels sang with great joy on that glorious day, bringing good tidings to the whole earth about the unutterable peace and joy that came on earth that no human tongue can express.

I longed to write to you on this feast as a sojourner on earth who has tasted estrangement.[1] I

---

[1] *Ġurba* is normally the Arabic translation of the Greek

became closer than many others to its secret meaning by which spiritual people live as sojourners and pilgrims seeking a better heavenly homeland (cf. Heb. 11:16). This is especially true since Nativity is the feast of estrangement and sojourners.

The first thing that the Lord Jesus suffered from on earth was estrangement, if ever estrangement is to be considered a form of suffering. It is undoubtedly so in one way, for He "came to His own, and His own did not receive Him" (John 1:11). The Lord Jesus was born a stranger, even to His mother and His mother's betrothed because they were astonished by all that was said about Him. His birth was atypical, and everything that surrounded His birth was mysterious. When He was born, His parents were on a journey, so He was born in a foreign land. Even if it was the land of His ancestors, they found no place in a house and His mother laid Him in a manger of cows, so He stayed over as a guest stranger even to the animal

---

word *xeniteía* (from *xénos*, 'stranger') which indicates the Christian "strangerness," the practice of being always sojourners.

world. There is no doubt that these things did not happen coincidentally or in vain, but there must be mysteries, wisdom, and divine teaching behind them that we must pay attention to.

The creative Creator of the universe was born a stranger on earth. Why? Because estrangement is the behavior of the sojourner, the stranger is always ready to leave, his heart is always attached to his homeland, and his face is fixed at all times towards his goal. He cannot be deterred by an enemy or even a friend, especially if he is aware of the certainty of his homeland and the glories that await him there.

The Lord Jesus was undoubtedly aware of His homeland. That is why He expressed to His disciples, “If you loved Me, you would rejoice because I said, ‘I am going to the Father,’ for My Father is greater than I” (John 14:28). As though He wants to say to them, “Rejoice with Me, because I will return to the bosom of the Father, from whom I came, to be glorified by the glory that I have with the Father before the foundation of the world.”

Were it not for the estrangement of the Lord

Jesus on earth, His saving message would have been lost for us humans—if we may make this assumption—for it is His estrangement that made Him refuse to establish an earthly kingdom even though He was certainly able to do so. His estrangement made Him not seek glory from people, nor look for a place to lay His head, nor expect everyone to understand or accept Him, for "all cannot accept this saying, but only those to whom it has been given" (Matt. 19:11).

The stranger must have different methods from those of others who are not from his homeland. This differentiation will certainly arouse aversion which may reach the point of hostility. That is why the Lord says to us, "If you were of the world, the world would love its own. Yet because you are not of the world, but I chose you out of the world, therefore the world hates you" (John 15,19). He warns us, "Woe to you if all men speak well of you" (Luke 6:26). Why? Because that means that, in our ways, we have become no longer strangers to those of the world, we have adapted to its way of life, think as it thinks, follow its ways, and aim for its goals. In this way, we lose our own goal, and we are now in danger of losing our authentic homeland.

If we experience alienation from our earthly homeland and find, in our exile, the comfort that we seek, the principles to which we rest, and the prosperity that we hope for, we will be exposed to the danger of ignoring the aspirations that live in the heart of our fellow citizens. Surely, we are all exposed to this danger.

Therefore, it is necessary for those who are away from their heavenly homeland to watch always over their heart in order to preserve its unextinguishable yearning towards their original country. They must continuously keep igniting the fire of this longing and never halt until they see this fire becoming a light that cannot be hidden under a basket (cf. Matt. 5:15), a light in which they walk and many follow them. But, nevertheless, they are strangers whose estrangement has not ended, since they are pilgrims traveling to their homeland, and their estrangement must end and they return to their homeland.

This is the message of the Lord Jesus, who came to cast fire on earth and only wants to kindle it (cf. Luke 12:49). He came to set the son against his father, the daughter against her mother, and the daughter-in-law against her mother-in-law. As we read in the Gospel of Matthew, "a man's enemies will be those of his own household" (Matt. 10:36). This is estrangement.

All that the Lord Jesus did was that He established a heavenly Kingdom on earth. And what a great gulf between Heaven and earth! Hence the estrangement of those who live on earth as citizens in the Kingdom of Heaven since the earth is not theirs and Heaven is their goal, and their true Father is in Heaven. He who called them up there has come to them from Heaven. "We beheld His glory, the glory as of the only begotten of the Father, full of grace and truth" (John 1:14). He stole their hearts and dazzled their eyes and took over their entire being. When He was lifted from them, He drew them up with Him, and they were no longer able to endure to be separated from Him. So, they started living with Him in their hearts, seeking those things which are above, where Christ is, sitting at the right hand of God (cf. Col. 3:1). Their souls on earth are longing to leave this body in order to settle with the Lord.

How magnificent is the estrangement that the Lord established by His birth on earth! If only we comprehended it well, we could preach estrangement in our life and death, in our going in and out, because the signs of estrangement from this world—if they appear upon us—are the greatest evidence in us and the strongest form of preaching that we are not of this world and that we are the children of the Kingdom.

Now, as your partner in the estrangement from this earth, I invite you to rejoice together in our God, who has sojourned for our sake, in order to call us to the Promised Land. He will lead us all the way to it, and so He will let us pass over the Red Sea of sins and the wilderness of this world. He will defeat for our sake our powerful and stubborn enemies; He will let us overcome those who vex us and possess a land we have not labored in cultivating. We will then eat the fruits of vineyards that we did not plant, abide in houses that we did not build, and live in a city whose walls are truth and whose doors are righteousness, whose sun is Christ, and whose joys have no end.

Blessed be God, the Father of our Lord Jesus Christ, the Father of mercies and the God of all comfort, to Him be glory forever in the Church.

13

Glory in Poverty

Dear Brethren of the *Bayt al-Takrīs*,[1]

Peace from God to your souls, and sincere supplications to Christ the Lord to support you with His grace in your life and perfect your struggle, patience, and faith.

On the occasion of the Nativity Feast, I would like to offer you a word that I derive from the mystery of Christ which motivates me and you to a life of consecration and poverty in its full meaning with renewed power beyond what the mind comprehends or imagines.

All that we can infer from our life so far is that

---

[1] *Bayt al-Takrīs* ('House of Consecration') in Ḥilwān, a suburb of the great Cairo, 25 kms from the Egyptian capital. Because of its remoteness and quietness, Father Matthew chose it to start a place where young celibates could live and serve the Church. This letter was written in 1967.

the call to walk after Christ requires vigilance in the journey to follow the voice of the shepherd, because the ascent on the road occurs suddenly. The one who does not pay attention will hit the rock of ascent and fall instead of ascending. In fact, those who have not faced the experience of their humiliation set for the ascent and are distracted from following the Lord by following the passions of their soul and body, the experience of humiliation becomes for them a cause of stumbling, slander, flight, and regression.

I can smell from behind these deserts and years the scent of your love that was born amid adversity. Your love has matured by trials, to be a sample of spiritual, non-emotional love, and a new testimony to the kind of ecclesial bonding and intimacy that those consecrated to God should live.

When I offer you the Nativity in these words, I present to you one of the mysteries of Christ, Heaven, the Virgin, and the angels, which cannot be transmitted to others before being experienced.

Heaven rejoiced at the Nativity. This was the clearest impression of the Nativity. For the first time in the life of all creation, the events of the earth became a joy for the heavenly ones. Because of the greatness and universality of joy, the angels came out of their eternal silence and shared with us their joy and revealed this wonderful news: "Behold, I bring you good tidings of great joy which will be to all people" (Luke 2:10).

Because of the strength and depth of its impact, the Gospel derives its name from this good news. And everyone who transmits this same Gospel—the good news of salvation announced at the Nativity—becomes like an "angel" of God or an "evangelist." As the Scriptures call the seven bishops in the book of Revelation, "To the angel of the church... write."

From here, brethren, we come to the heart of the message that God called you to, as consecrated persons for the Gospel or as angels of God who preach the good news of salvation and joy.

Thus, know that the sad person cannot transmit or pass on the joy to others, and those who have no reasons for true joy cannot convey with their emotions the salvific good news. The Gospel is a joyful force that transcends fear and all emotions teaching, "Do not be afraid, for behold, I bring you good tidings" (Luke 2:10).

Nativity is a power of joy, and the feast for those who rejoice in the Gospel. Nativity is thus a critical point in the consecrated life because it requires a heavenly joy that brings us out of our silence and sobriety, and even emotions, just like the joy that made the angels appear, so that we become evangelists of joy.

Therefore, every time we remember the Nativity, we must ask ourselves two questions: what did we do with this remembrance? And how did we react to its news? Indeed, the Nativity is not a mere remembrance, as the divine joy cannot be restrained to one of the human days and neither can words express the good tidings. The reality of the Nativity lives in the angelic heart; that is, in the heart of those who preach, as an eternal spring of joy and jubilation. The more we take from it, the more it increases; the more we give it, the more we are filled.

The person who lives facing the Gospel and

Christ lives on the day of His Nativity. That day, though it was recorded in history on a specific day, is in fact the Gospel of joy and unlimited salvation. It is God's day and not a human day, exceeding in the depth of its power and meaning a thousand years and more. One can say that the joy of the Nativity is equal to the joy of a thousand years of human joys if they were to be combined together without sadness.

The person who is consecrated to God is dedicated firstly and foremost to the Nativity. As Christ was born to die, the Christian must die to be born. Nativity for consecrated persons is both an end and a beginning of life. In other words, those who want to be born spiritually must first attain total death. Is not the birth of Christ an extraordinary act of self-abasement and *kénōsis*[2] that

---

[2] In Christian theology, *kénōsis* (lit. "the act of emptying") is the 'self-emptying' of the Logos, the second hypostasis of the Holy Trinity, who took the form of a servant. The word *kénōsis* comes from *ekénōsen* which is used in Philippians 2:7, "[Christ Jesus] emptied Himself [*ekénōsen*], taking the form of a servant, being born in the likeness of men" (RSV).

attains total death?

Here is the source of perfect joy. Has not this joyful salvation come to us through the complete poverty and *kénōsis* that the Lord has undertaken?

Here is the fountain of an overflowing eternal joy, which amazed the angels and commanded them with the power of the joyful tidings. The angel said, "Behold, I bring you good tidings of great joy" (Luke 2:10). So, in reaching total poverty, death, and renunciation of all glory, we acquire to ourselves the mystery of eternal joy that cannot be taken away from us. Every joy which lies on the gifts and glories of this world is taken away from us, but the joy of giving up the gifts and the glories of this world, what will take it away? When we attain the level of perfect joy that cannot be taken away, we will have reached the good news of the Nativity, and we will have become like the joyful angels of God. Then, we will give and will overflow, and our giving will have no end.

This is the mystery of the joyful tidings, and this is the power of the Nativity that stems from the mystery of *kénōsis* and the power of renunciation.

The Newborn is the Rich who became poor so that we can enrich ourselves with His poverty (cf. 2 Cor. 8:9). This is the exalted nature of Christ in its glory, supreme in its humility, overflowing with joy, jubilation, and gladness. When we realize the power of total poverty and death, we attain the glory of Christ's nature and its humility and sate ourselves from the joy that stems from its poverty. We will then water all people with glad tidings.

This is the mystery of the angelic joy given to people on the day of Nativity, and it is the same as the greatest critical point in the life of the consecrated person because the mystery of perfect joy does not stem except from the mystery of quintessential poverty. That is why the consecrated are put to an unbearable test if they abandon the mystery of poverty, meaning that they are looking forward to human glory or securing a future or bodily comfort.

The Virgin realized the depth of this experience when she accepted the signs of the mystery of the Nativity in her womb and praised: "My soul magnifies the Lord, and my spirit has rejoiced in God my Savior. For He has regarded the lowly state of His maidservant" (Luke 1:46–48). See how this wise saint related the ability to gleefully glorify God with humility. As for the secret of this new evangelical vision at its core, it was because she was filled with real humility that truly qualified her to be filled with Christ.

The mystery of praising God with the joy of the heart and soul is not given except for the one who is humble; it is this one whom God himself puts His seal upon.

Then, hear the Virgin continuing, "He has put down the mighty from their thrones, and exalted the lowly. He has filled the hungry with good things, and the rich He has sent away empty" (Luke 1:52–53). Here, Mary—the bearer of God's glory and humiliation—reveals the mystery of humility and the mystery of the satiety that she attained, whose meaning is found in her personal acceptance of Christ. That is to say that the presence of Christ in humanity is the mystery of elevation and satiety. And those who do not have

Christ will come down from their thrones and be dismissed empty-handed. In her canticle, the Virgin Mary refers to virginity with a concealed glimpse, as a state of hunger inside the consecrated person to God. It is not diverted by bodily satiety of any kind, nor deterred by pain, until it attains its fullness directly from God. Celibacy is a real, permanent hunger for God that can only be satisfied by the presence of God. For this reason, the Virgin Mary, when Christ came into her womb, felt full of bounties and a real sitting in the heavenly places. Mary, as a queen, was exalted in her poverty, reproaching those who were proud of their thrones and exalted themselves in their wealth. Here is an indication that the birth of Christ is a mystery that only those who are contrite could accept. As for the eyes that look to positions and power, they may rejoice at the Nativity but do not rejoice by it.

The genuinely poor one is the person who rejoices in real poverty and preaches it. Who ever heard that the rich rejoice in poverty? Or preach it? Those who give sermons, preach, and serve

Nativity diligently while looking in their hearts to fame that qualifies them for power, authorities, dignities, and worldly glories are trading Nativity as if writing a thesis on poverty to obtain a doctorate and a financial bonus.

Be well in the name of the Holy Trinity.

14

From the Manger to Calvary

Dearly Beloved Ones,

The grace of our Lord Jesus Christ be with you all. "The peace of God which surpasses all understanding" (Phil. 4:7) keep you faithful to Him and to the vocation for which you have been called for the praise of His name and the glory of His grace. May you be a beacon at the summit of His dwelling place.

I had written my first letter thinking that it would suffice. I felt, however, an urge to write again, asking the Lord Jesus Christ that my writings to you be not a burden on anyone. Let no one think that I have written it out of my long knowledge or understanding, for I am like a blind man groping his way and writing without knowing what I write. As such, by warning you against any sin, I find myself guilty of it. The blood of Jesus Christ, however, is able to thoroughly cleanse us from all sin (cf. 1 John 1:7) so we may be found blameless on that great Day of His coming which is at hand.

Purify yourselves, beloved brethren, together with myself, with the hyssop of the Holy Spirit. Put on raiment that befits meeting the Bridegroom for we have been bought at a price (cf. 1 Cor. 6:20) for that great Day having won our permission to enter, such that nothing remains but to prepare our raiment. Beware, then, that any of you should be slack in cleansing himself every day. Search your inner self to detect sins hidden deep within you. Expose them to the light of conscience lit by the knowledge of the Holy Spirit and the commandments of the Lord, which are an oil lamp for our path (cf. Ps. 118:105), indeed a sun in whose light we are being daily cleansed…

Today, you have begun upon the path leading to Calvary that starts from a manger. Bow down your heads, you who are chosen by God, that you may enter the cave of beasts. It is in there that your salvation lies, from such a contemptible place the sweet savor of your lives—the aroma of your humility—springs.

Go and seek out among the straw in a manger for animals and find out for yourselves a God who has abandoned Heaven and the splendor of the saintly angels to write for you the story of your salvation. He has sunk to the lowest dregs of humanity that He may not leave behind even a single human brother or sister whatsoever. He began His journey from among the beasts to secure His plan.

Before bearing the cross and following Christ, those who wish to become disciples have to be born first in a manger. It is there that their place lies, beneath all of humankind. Let them choose a place among the animals and once they manage to do that properly, they will realize that they have not been humble enough, for they will find that the Lord is more humble than they. Christ never ceases to say, "learn from Me, for I am gentle and lowly in heart" (Matt. 11:29).

You who love pure and untainted worship, our path begins where Christ began, with total renunciation, for this is the golden robe of humility. Contemplate the King of kings wrapped in rags on the day of his birth. Yearn for that royal garb as sons of the King that you may be able to become disciples to Him. Is it not enough for the disciple to be like his Master (cf. Matt. 10:25)?

Many are those who can wear the most elegant of clothing—impeccably clean and glitzy. But there is only one who can dress in rags—it is He, alone, who can bear the Cross.

Christ accepted being born in a manger as He wished to bear the Cross and accepted to die. He dressed in rags because He sought to conquer the world so that when the prince of this world comes, he would have nothing in Him (cf. John 14:30).

Christ had family and relatives in Bethlehem, for it was the city of David, yet He was there as a stranger. In the city of His father and mother, He was a stranger because He wished to become the Son of Man and a brother to all humanity. So long as we have fathers, brothers, sisters, or mothers, we are strangers to Christ, for all men are our relatives in accordance with the gospel reference to "your neighbor." "Love your neighbor as yourself" (Matt. 22:39), and "your neighbor" here includes the whole of humanity. As for him or her who loves father, mother, brother or sister, etc., "more than Me, is not worthy of Me" (Matt. 10:37).

Now, beloved ones, lift your eyes up to Bethlehem and acquire from it how to live as strangers. For wherever you are strangers, you are nearer to Heaven, since angels surround you from every side to save you. Commence with the manger to learn how to race backward, that is, behind the ranks. When you see that you have become the least of all, begin your journey, for this is your manger from which you will set out to Calvary.

If you become a snob and place some individuals behind you whom you consider sinners or slothful or who appear to you as unworthy or inferior, rest assured that your path is blocked. It will never lead you anywhere but from whence you began. But, if you were to see yourself as the least of all, you would immediately feel that you are striding with the power of Him who said, "and the last will be first" (Matt. 19:30); "whoever of you desires to be first shall be slave of all" (Mark 10:44); "just as the Son of Man did not come to be served, but to serve, and to give His life a ransom for many" (Matt. 20:28); "he who is greatest among you shall be your servant. And whoever exalts himself will be humbled, and he who humbles himself will be exalted" (Matt. 23:11, 12).

Make for yourselves golden robes from the rags in which Jesus was wrapped so that you may cover the ugliness of your bodies and members. Those who lack purity or sanctity of members or thoughts should choose for themselves a rag out of the few rags in which the Babe was wrapped. Let them lay it upon their body that they may be healed.

Renounce pride so humility may clothe you instead. Wrap yourselves with humility to cover yourselves from the shame of your thoughts.

Farewell in the name of the Holy Trinity!

15

The Joy That Christ Came to Bring on Earth

Dear Brethren,

Isaiah the prophet taught, "Truly, You are a God who conceals Himself, God of Israel, Savior!" (Is. 45:15).[1] This verse has not only caught my eyes or my mind, but my own life. In fact, I came to the same conclusion as Isaiah, but I wonder how Isaiah the prophet, who saw the Lord in a vision, said, "Woe is me, for I am undone! Because I am a man of unclean lips... For my eyes have seen the King, the Lord of hosts" (Is. 6:5), and then, later on, saying, "Truly, You are a God who conceals Himself, God of Israel, Savior!" (Is. 45,15).

[1] Translation is taken from The New Jerusalem Bible which better correlates to the Arabic translation on which the entire letter is built.

I also perceived God like this, I saw that He was concealed, though I outdid Isaiah the prophet in that I know the Lord Jesus and I live in the New Testament and thus I have seen Him with the faith of my heart. But despite this, I admit that He is still a concealed God.

You have heard the angels rejoicing in Heaven, who were seen in a clear vision by shepherds, who were neither anchorites, nor hermits, nor saints, and neither priests. They were shepherds who lived in the wilderness, who guarded the night watch nearby the village of Bethlehem. Then, suddenly appeared with the angel who brought the good tidings a multitude of heavenly host, praising in a clear audible voice which was recorded by mankind, amazingly and miraculously, as we now have it recorded—"Glory to God in the highest, and on earth peace, and joy in men!"[2] (Lk. 2:14).

---

[2] We adapted here the verse to a literal translation from the Smith and Van Dyck Arabic Bible used by Father Matthew the Poor because the version quoted and commented on by him differs from the common English translation.

Yet, despite all this, I say that Jesus remained a concealed God.

Jesus grew and became an adult. So, let me, for now, skip Bethlehem—though all my focus tonight should be centered on Bethlehem—and stand with Jesus on the Jordan River. We will see not angels nor archangels, but Heaven torn open and the Holy Spirit descending in bodily form like a dove and a voice not of angels, but a voice from the excellent glory, the Father's voice itself, expressing: "This is My beloved Son, in whom I am well pleased," or in another place "in You I am well pleased," as St. Luke the Evangelist recorded for us. Let me also go beyond Baptism and ascend the Mount of Transfiguration. I see again Heaven becoming earth, earth becoming Heaven, and the disciples Peter, James, and John. It is a vision of prophets witnessed by those disciples who recorded for us how the Lord was transfigured, not as a prophet but greater than a prophet. His face was shining like the sun and even His clothes became like light. Yet, despite that, I confess to you that Jesus remained and will remain the concealed God.

Tonight, all Christians celebrate the Nativity. If only we were given the insight to realize the great joy that is over the whole earth tonight! Churches and more churches rejoice and glorify, and peoples, nations, and tongues of every kind rejoice and glorify, and yet I say, "Truly, You are a God who conceals Himself, God of Israel." Despite mankind's joy, despite the voice of the angels, notwithstanding the voice of the Father who was heard three times,[3] and Heaven speaking with an audible voice hearable by humanity, He remained a concealed God.

Humanity has not responded in a real way to Heaven's voice, nor to the Lord's Transfiguration, nor to the voice of God the Father Himself, who said in the Transfiguration, "Listen to Him," and at the Jordan when He said to Him: "With You I am well pleased." Despite these impressive revelations, and though Christ Himself says about John

---

[3] These three instances were at Christ's Baptism, at the Transfiguration and when the Lord Jesus expressed to the Father, "Father, glorify Your name": "Then a voice came from Heaven, saying, 'I have both glorified it and will glorify it again'" (John 12:28).

the Baptist that "John the Baptist testified to Him," yet we find John sending to Jesus his disciples wondering, "Are You the Coming One, or do we look for another?" (Matt. 11:3). And as far as the disciples, Peter, James, and John, who witnessed the Transfiguration on the mount and everything that is transfigured in Christ, are concerned, you will find later that Peter denied Christ, John stood from afar at the Cross and had it not been for the presence of the Virgin, even John might have fled. Humanity has not responded adequately.

So, what is this joy at the Nativity? There are false joys—superficial, unreal joys. If we look closely at those who are rejoicing, we will find that they have a full stomach, "snug as a bug," with their pocket full of money, probably have got a recent promotion. In short, they are doing good, whether they are employees or priests, whether they are church servants or even the poorest poor. Look for the poorest person in any church on the feast day and ask him: "Is your stomach full?". He will reply, "Yes, thank God." Go and look for the hungry; we will not find them in the church! Look for the naked; we will not find them in the church! Look for the tired and the grieved; we will not find them in the church. Those who have been betrayed by the world and who have been oppressed by their fellow humans, you will find them tired and groaning, unable to rejoice.

Christ was born in Bethlehem, and Heaven rejoiced; now, we celebrate the birth of Christ on earth everywhere and we rejoice for Him. But in truth, Christ remained a God who conceals Himself. In all those who rejoice on earth, we cannot experience the newborn Christ, because all the joy is only apparent, coming out of hearts that have eaten and are filled. They rejoice from the abundance of food and satiety. I wonder, is there a broken heart that rejoices? If there is, then this is an eyewitness of the Nativity, for he or she has received a revelation from the God of Israel. In fact, we cannot say about our praises tonight that they are truly praises unless we can offer them while we are in the direst need and greatest distress.

One of the monks asked me: "Father, you say in one of your writings that we will be afflicted by many hardships and want. What is the meaning of 'want'?" I laughed to myself. We are not afflicted with want at present, because want means starvation, thirst, not finding clothes to cover or warm oneself. This monk wanted me to cross out the word 'want' because it is incomprehensible for him and he cannot swallow it.

Honestly, I cannot say that our praises tonight are genuine praises, though all of you chanted praises on the ambo, I cannot say that you have praised unless you entered into distress and tasted want, hardship, and pain. Only then will you really rejoice, give thanks and then praise. To those of you who experienced the above, I can say that the God of Israel is not concealed but is revealed.

As for those who praise harmonically to the sounds of music and all the instruments in the choirs in all the churches of the world, I cannot say that this is real praise, or real joy, or even an echo of the voices of the angels who taught us the Nativity praise. Every church at this time praises saying "Glory to God in the highest, and on earth peace, and joy in men." But what is this glorification of God, this feeling of peace on the land of misery, this joy felt in sad and suffering hearts? This praise is genuine and sincere when we can say it in our sorrows, pains, afflictions, and needs. But if we are filled, and warm, it is difficult for myself and for Christ who was born in Bethlehem, to say that this is real praise.

In fact, the whole world is still far from the truth of the Nativity because the truth of His birth remains hidden from the whole world. This is because, truly, as I told you from my experience, I felt in my life and believed in the verse of the prophet Isaiah that God is a "concealed God." In the years of my life, I learned to praise God from the depths of my heart and to praise with all boldness. When I experienced tribulation, my tongue stumbled, and praise came out stumbling from my tongue—if it came out—tinged with weeping, as a result of my pain. I am not necessarily talking about sufferings caused by a person, whoever he may be, but rather the tribulations of the soul that the Holy Spirit drives on us to harden and strengthen us.

This is what I learned from my experiences, in particular from one experience that made me often feel trapped within myself. When I felt in myself that I was in a period of abandonment and thought that the Lord had left me—though my thought was of course wrong—it was very difficult for me to praise, and my tongue stumbled and I could not rejoice, and the morning praise that I loved so much became meaningless on my tongue. In those days of distress, when I began to sing the praise that I used to sing every day at dawn tirelessly, *Piouoini entafmi* (O True Light), my tongue was silenced, and I found tears precede my tongue. My praise to Him had no thanksgiving, but only moaning and tears. At last, I understood that my previous praise was the praise of satiety, it was the praise of boldness and it was not genuine praise. I became certain that the Lord was opposing me for He did not like that, in times of trouble and pain, my tongue was withheld from praise and glorification.

My beloved ones, my brethren, I am not preaching now, for I am speaking out of years of experience, tears and tribulations. This is not a homily. I can pass on my experience teaching that if you cannot glorify God in the highest in the time of your distress, you will not be able to feel peace while the earth trembles under your feet. And if it is impossible for you to feel joy in moments of distress, Christ has not yet been born for you and has not yet appeared to you, and the God of Israel is still concealed for you.

Yet, on the day when your tongue frees itself from feeling sad because of your circumstances and tribulations, breaking forth in praising God in the highest, when you feel peace filling your heart despite all the difficulties and when you feel joy while you are among people who dislike you, then this joy you feel and this praise you sing will be the very same joy and praise of the angels at the Nativity.

Brethren, I am conveying to you my experience, a summary of a whole life, and not preaching. When the angels taught the shepherds the praise and glorification of the heavenly choirs, they taught them at midnight, and after the middle of the night a light shone, which means that they were in darkness. It is known, according to tradition, that Christ was born at midnight, and the vision was revealed in the midst of pain and cold, not in times of joy, but in times of distress. The Nativity praise is still concealed and many still sing it from their tongues, and they cannot weigh the depth of its words.

When we glorify God in truth, what is the meaning of glorification? We glorify God, meaning we elevate and exalt Him. God is glorified and He is the Father of glory, in that He is the Almighty who can elevate every creature to Him. When we glorify God, we must raise our weak nature to His highest with praise and glorification. We cannot glorify God if we are in a state of languor and unless we are in a state of inner ascension, mental ascension, a state of transfiguration, inner elevation, and spiritual warmth. We cannot truly glorify God unless we have been elevated in our inner being so that this inner elevation becomes a realization of the glory of God because God is glorious, elevated, exalted; that is, He is able to raise the lowly and the humble things and the humble people. Therefore, when we feel our humble state, we can, in the warmth of this humility and this poverty of spirit, raise our whole being by praising God—this is the real genuine praise. You cannot glorify God when you are in a state of boast or feeling pride or self-glory. Rather, you can glorify God in your humility and your poverty when you feel that your whole being is elevated as a sacrifice before God. This is giving glory to God.

Many ask, what does it mean to give glory to God? How is it ever possible for a person to give glory to God? God gives glory, and I give glory as well! I give glory to God with all my being when I rise from the dust, from the dunghill, from the dustbin of sin, from the dust of the animal instinct. Then, I raise my heart with the warmth of my spirit to praise my God in Heaven. This elevation is, beyond any doubt, a glorification of God. It is a revelation and a testimony that God is able to rise from the dunghill and He let us sit with the princes. When I raise my heart with my inner praise at any moment, this is the glorification of God.

And what is peace on earth? Earth was not and will never be a home of peace, ever. But she became so when she entered into contact and her face touched the body of the Lord Jesus Christ placed in the manger of beasts in the cave of Bethlehem. Then, peace necessarily came on earth. When we are in labor and distress, and Christ is truly born in our lives and our hearts, then we continuously and unceasingly contemplate in our heart His miraculous birth as well as His incarnation in us, to which we mystically take part all the time. When we feel that the Lord is in contact with us, then there will undoubtedly be peace on earth. No matter how difficult and hard the circumstances, if we can truly comprehend the birth of Christ spiritually, we will feel peace. This is peace: when the earth trembles and shakes under my feet, I feel peace because the Lord is with me and He is in my being. I feel tranquility because the Lord came down to the earth and blessed it.

The demons once appeared to a monk and disturbed him from sleep, and he heard the sound of a war trumpet. So, he went out looking from his window and said, "What is this? Is it war?" Satan replied, "Yes, it is war, O monk. Either you fight or you throw your weapon!"[4] This is an allegorical story. The monk, the hermit, and any person who has withdrawn from the world is in constant war with the forces of darkness who are able to shake the earth and the air around you and disturb you in a very deceptive manner, without reason, making your soul upset and deeply distressed. This happens if Christ is not resurrected in your being and you do not feel His true birth and His being in contact with this earth. In such a case, you will experience fatigue and misery. But when you feel this peace, when you feel the birth of Christ, all these pains become like smoke, as when you read in the ascetical literature that the monk makes the sign of the Cross and says, "May the Lord rebuke you, Satan," and Satan becomes like smoke.

Indeed, we cannot feel peace on this earth, the land of misery, unless we have the Prince of Peace

[4] Father Matthew is referring here to an apophthegm of the Desert Fathers which is found in the Arabic collection of *Bustān al-Ruhbān* (apophthegm 701).

with us and unless our eyes are focused, not on a theological notion that says that He was incarnated and descended onto earth, but on the living and unshakable truth that the Christ God came down into contact with our earth eternally. Hence why until now the earth is called "His footstool." When we feel this and when we are attached to Him, we will have peace on this earth.

As for the joy, many people illude themselves to be in joy, though they are not. Brethren, joy is not the result of satisfaction, nor even spiritual satisfaction. My beloved, this is not the joy that Christ came to give to the world. When you pray or intercede for others in prayer and feel joy, this is not the joy that Christ came to give on earth. Neither when you fast and feel your throat dry, your stomach completely empty, your saliva bitter and dry, and your mouth emanates an unpleasant smell, and then you rejoice because you offer fasting as a sacrifice to God. Moreover, nor when you live in a community with good and pleasant brethren who love, bless, help and support each other at all times and on every occasion, so you say, "Oh my! How lucky I am" and rejoice. This also is not the joy that Christ came to cast on earth. Lastly, not either when you are in a spiritual ecstasy after a divine sight, even if it is the Lord God Himself, such that your heart is filled with joy. This is not the joy that Christ came to give.

The joy that the angels announced on the day of the Lord's birth is the joy that can prevail over sorrow, the joy that can be born in the depths of human sadness; it is such joy I talk about. On the day when you are in unbearable stress and sadness, in the midst and depth of sadness, and feel inner joy, and are consoled know that this is the joy that Christ came to give. It is a rare joy. No creature, nor satisfaction, nor grace, nor talent can give it to you, except the Lord Jesus Christ Himself because He was born in the grief of the earth and the heart of its sorrows and sins. While we were still sinners, Christ was born for us and died (cf. Rom. 5:8). That is, Christ was born in the depth of grief, in the depth of death, and in the depth of human suffering. So, when the angels in Heaven announced the joy that was on earth at the time of Christ's birth, this was a joy that was extremely precious for the earth, because it could not exist without His birth nor His presence. When Christ is born amid our sorrows and distress, and amid our dryness and coldness, joy is born. This is the joy that the angels announced: "Glory to God in the highest, and on earth peace, and joy in men."

Brethren, we live in the realm of the verse, "Truly, You are a God who conceals Himself, God of Israel." We experience in our small community the depth of this concealment. Our life is hidden in Christ and has no appearances, and nothing more than this is evident that our spiritual life grows without external appearances, without titles, or positions, or prestige. Our life grows secretly, far from the appearances of false joys. Beyond the distracting world, we grow, walking the long distance of our life, facing little by little eternity.

Printed in Great Britain
by Amazon